Does
PROTOTYPING
HELP OR HINDER
GOOD REQUIREMENTS?

*What are the best practices
for using this method?*

FREEDOM TOWEH

Order this book online at www.trafford.com
or email orders@trafford.com

 www.trafford.com

North America & international
toll-free: 1 888 232 4444 (USA & Canada)
fax: 812 355 4082

Because of the dynamic nature of the Internet, any web addresses or links contained in this book may have changed since publication and may no longer be valid. The views expressed in this work are solely those of the author and do not necessarily reflect the views of the publisher, and the publisher hereby disclaims any responsibility for them.

Our mission is to efficiently provide the world's finest, most comprehensive book publishing service, enabling every author to experience success. To find out how to publish your book, your way, and have it available worldwide, visit us online at www.trafford.com

ISBN: 978-1-4907-9652-9 (sc)
          978-1-4907-9651-2 (e)

Print information available on the last page.

Trafford rev. 08/09/2019

Does Prototyping help or hinder good requirements? What
are the best practices for using this method?

By

Dr. Freedom Toweh, D. Comp Sc, Msc, ISSM

ABSTRACT

Prototyping does help good requirements and some of the best practices for using this method of approach include some design alternatives and creating a subset. One of the primary reasons for creating a prototype is to obviously resolve the unknown at the early stage of the development process. There are several beneficial reasons for creating prototypes, but this book will examine some of those which include requirements validation, design exploration and to also explore some of the best practices for using this method of approach. Without contradiction prototypes cost money and time, but it equally reduces the risk of software project failure. Prototyping can improve the quality of requirements and specifications that are provided to developers. This book will critically examine the various benefits of prototyping with a reflection on whether prototyping helps or hinder good requirements?

Does Prototyping Help or Hinder Good Requirements? What are The Best Practices for Using this Method?

A software prototype is a partial, possible, or preliminary implementation of a proposed new product according to Wiegers and Beatty (2013). Poor requirements are in most cases the major cause of late products with so many bugs and design flaws. An effective prototyping process can reduce cost and improve customer satisfaction and delight (Wilson, 2010). A prototyping with an effective approach can also be used to validate and extract assumptions and requirements that exist among the product team.

It is important to understand that requirements may have unwanted side effects before the creation of the final product which only a prototype can expose. Arnowitz, Arent and Berger (2007) suggested that too often in the software process, design and creation are crammed into the late stages when there is little time available for prototyping and validation, thus leading to high-risk software development.

This book will first cover a review of the literature, and secondly it will explore the significance of prototyping and examine its benefits.

OVERVIEW

There are different types of steps that could lead to the successful completion of a software project. And one of such steps is the creation of a software prototype. Prototyping resolves uncertainties at the early stage of the development process. It is also important to fully understand and communicate very effectively why you are creating the prototype and your ideal use of it after it has been evaluated. The key factor really is its expression to allow the users of the software to evaluate the developer's proposals of the said product design instead of trying to interpret the design by means of mere description.

In the 60s and 70s, the idea was to build first and then later work out any type of inconsistencies that were detected between the design and implementation phases. The problem with this type of thinking was that it was a symbol of higher software costs that led to overall poor estimates of time and cost.

Prototyping detects inconsistencies at the early stages of the development phase which can be corrected early to save costs and time. But the reality is that prototyping helps to avoid bigger expense, and the trouble of having to change a finished software product.

One very critical aspect of software development is to ensure that you formally agree with your client on the requirements and the scope of the project, which is critical to the implementation of prototyping.

And as such this book will examine some of its major purposes which includes requirements validation, design alternatives, and the creation of a subset that could possibly expand to become an ultimate product at the end. However, some of the best practices for using this approach, and the different types of prototypes as related to good requirements will also be examined.

SIGNIFICANCE OF PROTOTYPING

Let me reiterate by saying that a prototype is basically a sample of what your software will look like upon release. In every project for example taking software development as a case study, you simply start by defining clear business goals or objectives with a vision of what you want to achieve. This helps the users to understand the goals and direction of the development process.

'During requirements development the software concept becomes tangible through the creation of several versions of a user interface prototype and a user manual. This approach facilitates gathering the best possible set of requirements, lays a foundation for excellent architecture work, streamlines the project by eliminating the time-consuming detailed requirements documents, and keeps user documentation off the critical path' (McConnell, 1997).

Validate requirements

Prototyping is advantageous in validating some of the technical decisions that may arise at an earlier stage of development. For example, you may want to perform a feasibility study or even measure performance well ahead of your project. The concept or the implementation of a prototype will obviously guide you to an expected end before you actualize your main system. 'Kanovich (2014) suggested that prototyping refers to software, mobile or web application development approach where instead of freezing requirements and building a solid project base, the developer builds a working version which allows you to engage and interact with the system, get a feel for the user experience and interface, and provide very quick feedback'.

It is important to note, and understand that when you build out a prototype in your budget, it helps to avoid unforeseen later cost. The point here is that when you make an upfront spending investment on prototyping, you save yourself development costs and resources by trying to avoid future mistakes that might occur. Prototyping could be used as a requirements tool where by it helps in finding errors and omissions, assessing the quality of the requirements and its accuracy including areas of obtaining agreements.

With the implementation of prototyping approach, you can explore the ideas that you have before you carry out an investment on them. Let's remember that in this process, prototype saves you valuable resources and time before you finally take on investing in the design and technology of your project.

Organizations such as Microsoft, Disney and others of all types do use prototypes. Boeing for example builds digital prototypes of its aircraft to avoid design conflicts before its part are manufactured.

The concept works

In a given project, there is this tendency that the development team might disagree on the future direction of the project. And so the question is how you do get everyone in the team to see the direction and play along? Well you can use a prototype as an evidence of proof to shine some light into the ideas as to whether they have any future viability or rather value. Bottom line is that it can help to express or illustrate its qualities in an iterative way whereby the team members can begin to get motivated.

DESIGN ALTERNATIVE AND EXPECTATION GAP

Prototyping is used as a design tool which allows stakeholders to explore user interaction from different angles of perspectives. It can also demonstrate and evaluate potential technical approaches as well. And more importantly, is that it can be used to affirm the developer's true understanding of the requirements before the real construction takes place.

I will argue that without an adequate customer's involvement in a project, the outcome at the end of such a project could create an expectation gap. And this could come as a surprise to stakeholders which is not the good news for the entire process because portions of your requirements might be unclear and perhaps uncertain to customers. Requirements do also get out of data because of environmental changes that do occur in businesses, it is therefore important to recommend an ongoing interaction with customers to close such expectation gap.

Such closure however, will help the developer to closely build in alignment to the customer's needs. Prototyping is a very powerful approach to introduce all of the customer's important contact from the perspective of 'requirements' from the customer which can obviously reduce such an expectation gap. Prototyping excels in shaping the requirements at the early stage of a development process before an expensive development effort begins and as mentioned earlier, software prototyping takes a tentative step into the solution space.

'Prototyping makes the requirements more real, brings use cases to life, and closes gaps in the developer's and customers understanding of the requirements. Prototyping puts a mock-up or an initial slice of a new system in front of users to stimulate their thinking and catalyze the requirements dialog. Early feedback on prototypes helps stakeholders arrive at a shared understanding of the system's requirements which reduces the risk of customer dissatisfaction. (Wiegers and Beatty, 2013)'.

As a subset creation

And among other reasons that are beyond the scope of this book, prototypes are also a valuable tool for the creation of a subset of a product that can expand or rather grow to become the desired product. And as mock-ups it can demonstrate the functional options that the likely user may have available. The argument without much contradiction is that a prototype can be used as a construction tool as a functional implementation of the end-product's subset that can later on be elaborated into the full product through various steps of small-scale development cycles.

HYPOTHESIS

Prototyping is seen as risky because of its costs of time and money. Prototyping evaluation is related to usability, and a proof-of-concept prototype may not use tuned algorithms, or it may lack security layers that could reduce the ultimate performance.

Poor requirements are in most cases the major cause of late products with so many bugs and design flaws. An effective prototyping approach can be used to validate and extract assumptions and requirements that exist among the product team.......and then reduce cost and improve customer's satisfaction.

Why prototyping?

Prototyping excels in shaping the requirements at the early stage before an expensive development effort begins. Prototyping does help good requirements, and as such provides several valuable benefits such as design alternatives, validates requirements, creates a subset, and among others it enables end-user documentation and test plans to be developed in parallel with architectural design, and implementation.

It is important to understand that prototyping is an iterative process which is part of the analysis phase of the systems development life cycle. And as such it helps the analyst to develop an initial set of system requirements. Its use has also become widespread and part of that is because it increases the quality and amount of communication between the developer, analyst, and the end user.

It is reasonably strategic to note that instead of holding on to the requirements before a design or coding can proceed, a prototype can be built to fully understand the requirements. And this can help the client to understand the requirements of the desired system. May be 'prototyping idea' can also be very helpful for complicated and large systems that lacks manual process for determining the requirements.

User involvement

Prototyping helps the user(s) to see and interact which helps them to provide a better feedback and specifications. The user's knows the problem domain much better than those on the development team, and as such a sound interaction can lead to a final product that has greater tangible and intangible quality.

Some of the other advantages of prototyping includes higher user satisfaction, future system enhancement, errors can be detected at early process, better user feedbacks which can lead to good solutions, potential missing functionality can be easily identified, reduction of required manpower, and time and cost reduction. Realistically, prototyping can always improve the quality of specifications and requirements that are provided to developers. And as such an early determination of what the user may need can obviously result to faster and cheaper software.

A management information system (MIS) managers' survey in fortune 1000 companies indicated that there are four prototyping methodologies that are in use today when compared to the traditional systems development life cycle. And as mentioned they are illustrative, functional, simulated and evolutionary.

Table 1 below compares the prototyping phases to the Traditional phases as argued by Atwater, Lantz, Hunter & co (n.d).

Table (1)

Prototyping VS Traditional Project

Prototyping Phases	Traditional Phases
Determine Feasibility	Determine Feasibility
Study Present System	Study Present System
Define Prototype	Define Requirements
Build Prototype	Design Program
Exercise Prototype	Test Acceptance, Test train users
Convert	Convert
Install	Install

In comparing the prototype approach to the traditional methodology of how it is usually done, the use of prototyping approach does require less time for a project to be completed because the work of most of the phases are concurrently done, unless the amount of resources that are used in the prototyping approach is significantly below expectation. In information systems for example, prototyping does not only provide a continuation of phases, but it does provide more than iteration phases.

'Gremillion and Pyburn (1983) noted that a number of companies report indicated that the total systems development costs by the prototype approach are usually less than 25% of the costs with the traditional approach'.

Disadvantages

Prototypes are not emphatically complete systems, and that is because many of the details are usually not implemented in the prototype. And so, the goal really is to provide a system with an overall functionality. That being said, let's look at some of the main disadvantages of prototyping.

Poor analysis

It can be argued that developers focus on a limited prototype can create some type of distraction from giving a proper analysis of the entire project. And in addition, it can open the door for incomplete specifications that can lead to poor engineered completed projects that are terribly hard to maintain. The issue of incomplete or inadequate problem analysis may also arise because it can lead to the idea of taking better solutions for granted.

- The scope of the problem may expand beyond the original plans because the methodology may perhaps increase the complexity of the system.

- Some users may expect the performance of the main system to be the same as the prototype.

- The tendency that developers may become too attached to their prototype.

Software architecture and design

The argument however is that the design process that is used for the identification of a subsystem that makes up a system and the framework for the subsystem control and communication is known or can be referred to as the architectural design (Menasce et al, 1995). On the other hand, the output of such a design process is referred to as the description of the software architecture.

The fact of the matter is that an architectural design is a type of a creative process....so therefore the process is always different depending however on the type of system that is being developed. Nevertheless, there is a common number of decisions that span all design processes.

To analyze an architectural design for its desired quality attributes, I may have to examine some of the architectural design decisions which relates to the type of approach that will be used to structure the system. For example, what types of control strategies are needed to be used? How will the architectural design be evaluated and documented? What are the processes for the system distribution? How will it be decomposed into modules etc. etc. Let's look at the architectural styles for example: An architectural model of a system can conforms to a generic architectural model. Most systems that are large are heterogeneous and as such they do not follow one single architectural style.

Issues of common interest

There are some common issues that are found in concurrent software design as well which are also significant. Issues such as engineers having to think that object-oriented analysis of a concurrent hardware modules may guarantee a good concurrent software design which is supposed to deliver a flexible concurrent software architecture. Perhaps it could be that the concurrent architecture is reasonably hard to understand. Most.... if not all designs really do not have a clear distinction between the code that is controlling the system resource operation and the code that is performing the system resource concurrency. And finally, it could also be that the team's member does not have the required experience in concurrency design.

Why architectural design of concurrent systems is difficult?

I do believe from the standpoint of an architectural design that software architecture is the fundamental framework that is viable for the structuring of the system. The architectural design of concurrent systems seems to be difficult for several reasons, but partly because as unlike architectural design, the fundamental structural choices which are made can be more costly to manage once they are implemented. A more effective approach of utilizing single-based architectural description language (ADLs) can also be an issue.

But let's not forget that an architectural design of concurrent systems could be difficult because it has to be built on a solid foundation. Any multi-threaded system can be a concurrent system.... however, and for the most part, most systems do end up with only few engineers that can understand and maintain the fragile concurrent kernels. It could be that the understanding of the system concurrency is very low. It can also be argued that the presentation of a full picture of how the system concurrency design will work is not fully presented until the alpha or beta stage which is.... a lack of good approach to communicate the software design. Schmidt et al (1999) argues that architectural design of concurrent system is difficult due to the differences between standalone and networked application architecture.

Patterns in software architecture

Software architecture according to Buschmann, Sommerlad, Rohnert & Stal (1996) is a description of the subsystems and components of a software system and the relationships among them. They argued that the software architecture of a system is an artifact which is the result of the software design activity. Patterns do shine in the dark corners of software architecture design; because they can take you to the outside pedestrian object design methods (Buschmann, 1996).

Patterns are vitally important for constructing high-quality software architecture because one of its objectives is to build software systems with predictable non-functional properties. So therefore, it can also be considered to build on the principles that are essential for the development of software with reuse including design for change etc.

The question that comes to mind, however, is that of how patterns relate to existing design methods and analysis. Coplien (1996) indicated that designers do try to look to patterns first for their design solutions which were one of the fears that he harbored with regards to patterns. He argued that so many design problems can be solved by other well- known paradigms and that designers should attempt to take on those in their toolkits instead of just trying to use the most recent tools.

Complien's argument was quite clear and commendable. Yet, knowing that the choice of concurrency architecture does have a great impact on the design and performance of multi-threaded software as a whole seem to be very interesting. Perhaps because it is surprisingly true to some level of understanding that well-structured, responsive and efficient concurrent software can be hard to design.

It can be argued that patterns do cover only a small hole in the design space.The broader design space lends itself well to the common techniques of well-known paradigms. Thus, we should seek to use those paradigms where they fit as indicated by Buschmann (1996). If we can bring our expectations to control, we can obviously implement the use of both patterns and methodologies to the best of our advantage.

The construction of quality software revolves around several guidelines and steps that are provided by methodologies while the implementation of patterns addresses the needs of each specific problem.

A close look will reveal that patterns as pointed out by Buschmann & Summerlad,1996) complements the existing analysis and design methods with a set of concrete techniques for solving very specific but recurring design problems. Nevertheless, the implementation of both methodologies and patterns will not be a solution to all the design problems that you will have to resolve; rather you will have to deal with some on your own.

CONCLUSION

The question of whether prototyping helps good requirements is not contestable. Prototyping helps good requirements despite of some of its own risks of cost time and money. Of course, a stakeholder may see a throwaway prototype which in his or her mind may think that it is almost complete. But the fact is that a throwaway prototype is not meant for production use, rather it is just a simulation or an experiment.

Prototyping provides a very powerful set of techniques that can really reduce development costs, ensure the production of high-quality products, ensures an effective requirements process, and a reduction in the required manpower. And in addition, prototypes are also very good means for designing good human computer interface systems. Let me conclude by saying that prototyping obviously helps good requirements.

REFERENCES

Arnowitz, J; Arent, M; & Berger, N. (2007). Effective Prototyping for Software Makers

Morgan Kaufmann Publishers

Atwater, Lantz, Hunter & CO (n.d). The prototyping Methodology. Retrieved from

www.manageknowledge.com

Buschmann, F; Meunier, R; Rohnert, H; Sommerlad, P, & Stal, M. (2009). Pattern- Oriented Software Architecture:

A System of Patterns: John Wiley & Sons Publication Chichester NY

Gremillion, Lee L; & Pyburn (1983). Breaking the Systems Development Bottleneck:

Harvard Business Review, Vol. 61, No 2 p.133

Kanovich, V. (2014). Prototyping-Benefits and Best Practices: Corporate Blog

Retrieved April 22, 2015 from http://blog.sphereinc.com/201404/protyping-benefits

McConnell, S. (1997). Software Project Survival Guide: How to be Sure Your First Project

Isn't Your Last. Microsoft Press

Smith, M.F. (1991). Software Prototyping: Adoption, Practice and Management

McGraw-Hill, London

Schmidt et al (1999). Pattern-Oriented Software Architecture vol 2, Patterns for concurrent and networked objects: Wiley publications

Wiegers, K. & Beatty, J. (2013). Software Requirements: Best Practices

Microsoft Press Publications

Wilson, C. (2010). User Experience: Re-Mastered- Your Guide to Getting the Right Design

Elsevier Morgan Kaufmann Publishers

Printed in the United States
By Bookmasters